Some go Through – Some go Over !

Under the direction, and with the cooperation, of Army Ordnance—Cadillac has developed, and is building, what have proved to be two of the most effective pieces of armament in the Arsenal of Democracy.

One is the M-5 Light Tank—a fast, quick, highly-maneuverable weapon, armed with a high velocity, 37 mm. cannon. This tough, speedy, hard-hitting tank is one of America's great "surprise weapons"—ideal for upsetting enemy formations. Like a speedy halfback, it darts through the slightest opening in the line, or "runs the ends," as the need may be. It is almost as fast as a motor car.

The other is the M-8 mounting the Army's 75 mm. Howitzer cannon. Utilizing the same chassis as the M-5, it gives to demolition artillery a degree of mobility it has never known before. With this weapon, big guns can follow their targets—keep the position from which they can do the most good.

The two units that give these weapons their power and maneuverability were developed by Cadillac in peacetime: the Cadillac V-type engine and the Hydra-Matic transmission.

The quickness with which these peacetime units were sent to war not only attests their inborn quality of design and construction— but it indicates the splendid manner in which Army Ordnance has utilized the nation's resources to astound the world with its armament program.

 LET'S ALL

AMERICAN TANKS
of World War II

Thomas Berndt

MBI Publishing Company

To my dear, departed friend, James Harry Canning,
whom I miss so much and will never forget

First published in 1994 by MBI Publishing Company,
PO Box 1, 729 Prospect Avenue, Osceola, WI
54020-0001 USA

© Thomas Berndt, 1994

MBI Publishing Company books are also available
at discounts in bulk quantity for industrial or sales-
promotional use. For details write to Special Sales
Manager at Motorbooks International Wholesalers
& Distributors, 729 Prospect Avenue, PO Box 1,
Osceola, WI 54020-0001 USA.

Library of Congress Cataloging-in-Publication Data

Berndt, Thomas
    American tanks / Thomas Berndt.
       p. cm. — (MBI Publishing Company
       enthusiast color series)
    Includes index.
    ISBN 0-87938-930-3
    1. Tanks (Military science)—United States. 2.
World War, 1939-1945—Equipment and supplies.
I. Title. II. Series: Enthusiast color series.
UG446.5.B377   1994
623.7'4752'0973—dc20   94-5254

On the front cover: The early M4A1 with standard
75mm gun owned by Jacques Littlefield. Tom Berndt

On the frontispiece: Cadillacs wartime magazine
advertisement promoting its contribution to the M5 and
M8 light tanks for the US war effort.

On the title page: Lineup of American tanks of World
War II, from left: M4 Sherman, M5A1 light tank, and
M3A1 light tank. Tom Berndt

On the back cover: The M2A1 half-track. Tom Berndt

Printed in China

Contents

Acknowledgments

The military vehicle hobby began in the late 1960s, and quickly led to the emergence of a national organization, the National Military Vehicle Collectors Association. In the mid-1970s, another organization, the Military Vehicle Preservation of Independence, Missouri, was formed. This in turn led to the development of many state or local chapters of both organizations throughout the United States.

Well-organized local chapters, with the national organization's help, sponsor a national show each year in the continental United States. Transporting a military vehicle cross-country is time consuming and expensive but is a great delight to club members, some of whom will actually drive their vehicles to a show. It has been my privilege to meet many of these fine people over the years. Everyone has different interests and vehicles; consequently, the exposure has been overwhelming for me. You'd be hard-pressed to find a more pleasant, fascinating, and diverse group of people.

Much has been written on military vehicles, particularly the smaller vehicles. After my first publication, *Standard Catalogue of U.S. Military Vehicles 1940–1965* (Krause Publications, 1993), and the fantastic, positive response to it, I felt new information should be made available to the public on the larger vehicles, particularly heavy armor.

There are many collectors of these vehicles in the United States who undertake the tremendous challenge of buying, restoring, and maintaining an armored vehicle. These vehicles were designed to perform a specific function, and ease of maintenance and care was secondary. Often, a tank can require six to eight hours of maintenance for every hour it is operated. Just the cleaning can be a chore on tracked vehicles driven off-road. A great deal of work goes into keeping a beautifully restored military vehicle in top shape.

Over the years, the collectors of armor have persevered, and now beautiful, full restorations—interior and exterior—are being done on armored vehicles, including both large and small tanks. This book is an opportunity for everyone to see these fine vehicles owned by collectors, and realize that people do in fact own and enjoy them just as any other car, truck, or other collectible vehicle.

I would like to thank the following people for sharing their time, labor, and vehicles to make this book possible. Their contributions are sincerely appreciated by myself, all the readers, and other collectors: Frank Buck; George DeBonis; Ralph Doubek; Don Douda; Jim Fitzgerald; Andre Gibeau; Don Gunderson; Roy Hamilton; George Hilton; Reg Hodgson; John Jay; Jacques Littlefield; Joe McClain; Bill Nahmers; George Rabuse; Grant Rabuse; Fred Ropkey; Jack Terrill; Sloan and John Upton; Henry Venetta; Robert Wichmann; Skip Worvel; David Wright.

I would also like to thank my wife and family for their love and patience, and Marilyn Thompson for technical assistance in the production of this book.

M1917A1
This M1917A1 is an extremely rare American World War I tank, a US-built version of the French Renault FT17. Few survive today, and this one was found years ago in northwestern Minnesota, where it had been used for log skidding. Owner Joe McLain has completely restored it and it runs as good as it looks.
Tom Berndt

The Rapid Development of Tanks— And Their Legacy

World War I was believed to be the war to end all wars. Little did anyone know what would happen twenty years later all over the world.

The late 1930s brought turbulent times to the world order. Germany and Japan were attacking and occupying nations along their frontiers for political gain and natural resources. Technology in automotive and weaponry systems advanced greatly during these years, and both countries used this new technology to their advantage.

Germany and Japan began their armament programs in the early 1930s with great secrecy. The United States, on the other hand, did little weapons development until just a few years before the start of the Second World War. Consequently, when war broke

M4A1 Sherman Medium Tank
The American armored hero of World War II, the M4 Sherman tank. This early M4A1 was fitted with the standard 75mm gun seen here with the later mantlet. This M4A1 is owned by Jacques Littlefield.
Tom Berndt

out in the late 1930s, the German and Japanese equipment was far superior to anything that the United States had at that time.

In the mid-1930s, the United States was still using light tanks from World War I alongside horse-mounted cavalry. In the new war, however, mobility and speed were the keys to victory. Newer and better vehicles were needed to keep up with the enemy.

Cavalry, because of its mobility, was the natural choice for the armored corps of the US forces. During the 1930s, horse-drawn equipment was slowly phased out in favor of the rapidly improving automotive and truck units. The first vehicles were civilian wheeled trucks converted to all-wheel drive. Then came armor, followed by the development of the half-tracked truck.

Light tanks came next with the early M1 and M2 combat cars, which later evolved into the popular M3 radial engine tank and M5 twin V-8 engine tank. The next step was medium tanks, and these developed into the M3 Lee and, using the basic design and chas-

First in the automotive industry
to fly the Navy "E" with two stars,
Fisher has also been awarded the
Army-Navy "E" for its ahead-of-
schedule tank production.

"Better than a rabbit's foot!"

Our fighting men have a tough job to do, and they are doing it. They are finding out, in all parts of the world, what they have to work with. They are the best judges of the weapons with which American industry is supplying them.

They know just how fast the General Sherman M-4 medium tank will go — how accurate that seventy-five is — and whether or not direct hits will bounce off the armor plate.

The test of action in actual service gives them the final answer — the only one that matters.

Here at Fisher, we want to make sure it's the *right* answer. That's

why we give our tanks, bombers, and anti-aircraft guns the best we've got in us. We're using every craft we've mastered, every special skill we've developed — and they add up to an impressive number — to give our armed forces that all-important edge.

Come the pinches, craftsmanship always counts. And it's only natural that our fighting men should rate such craftsmanship as "better than a rabbit's foot."

armament
~~BODY~~ BY *Fisher*

sis, the M4 Sherman series, the most well-known tank even today.

All of this development took place in just a few short years before December 7, 1941. Many people today still consider World War II to be America's finest hour as everyone worked together so hard and so efficiently to defeat the aggressive enemies of democracy.

Much of today's basic automotive technology can be traced to the mechanical designs and the manufacturing technology of World War II tanks and other armored vehicles. Ford-built tank engines had gear-driven overhead camshafts, aluminum-alloy engine blocks, cylinder heads with hemispherical combustion chambers, and much more. Some of these advances weren't seen for thirty-five years after World War II in cars and trucks. The Continental aircraft engines, on the other hand, are still used today with the same designs and parts. They were so well built, even today NOS (new-old-stock) parts are still used—forty-five years later!

The diesel engine was a greatly misunderstood powerplant during World War II, and the United States used few of them. The M3A1 Stuart tank had a Guiberson radial diesel but only several hundred were ever built; the M4A2 Sherman used twin 6-71 Detroits, but these were given to England and used by associated countries. The United States used these diesel tanks for training, although a few were used in combat. The Germans never used diesel engines in their tanks; all were powered by V-12 Maybach gas models.

The tanks and armored fighting vehicles (AFVs) shown in this book are examples of beautifully restored US armored vehicles of World War II that are in collectors' hands today. Many of them have gone through ground-up restorations and are literally new in every way. Often they are in better condition than when they left the factory. They cover all areas of armored vehicles: half-tracks; light, medium, and heavy tanks; armored cars; and scout cars. Even some rare prototype vehicles exist yet today.

1

Scout Cars

White M3A1 Scout Car

One of the earliest armored vehicles of the World War II period was the White M3A1 scout car first created in 1938 by the White Motor Company. Based on a commercial truck chassis, it was an easily built vehicle.

The White was basically an armored truck with a face-hardened 1/4in armor-plated body. Plates were bolted on individually with a series of reinforcing steel brackets and dowels underneath; hardened armor screws of several lengths held the body together. Floors were made of heavy steel and sheet

White M3A1 Scout Car
In the driver's compartment of the scout car, folding canvas-covered seats for the driver and commander with the driver's gloves, goggles, and canteen show how simple the interior was. The instrument panel shows the gauges, voltmeter, glovebox, and data plate. Vacuum wiper motors are mounted below the removable windshield glass. Three support legs hold up the 1/2in windshield armor when not used. On the left, the armor screws that hold the body and armor plate are well shown. Jack Terrill

metal: aluminum diamond plate was used in early models; later units had steel diamond plate. Seats, cabinets, and radio mounts made up the spartan interior.

At the front of the vehicle was a spring tension roller, designed for "unditching" the truck when it went into a deep ditch with steep sides. The roller system prevented the front end from becoming stuck in the bank of dirt. Tow hooks were mounted just behind it for pulling the truck when needed.

Armored shutters covered the radiator for combat and could be opened or closed when needed. A lever with stops for certain positions was located on the floor below the dash by the passenger's right foot.

The front fenders were heavy sheet metal and the hood was a butterfly type opening on each side. The windshield was made of two panels of 1/2in armor plate with vision slots on each side.

The battery box was located in the right side of the vehicle with an armored cover. On the outside of the unit, pioneer tools—an ax, shovel, and pick—were strapped under each door with canvas or leather straps. Each rear fender had a cabinet with a lid over it for storing ammunition, section tools, and spare parts.

The doors featured hinged upper halves that folded down. The top halves contained vision slots with covers on the inside. Side curtains with pyrolin windows covered the upper door halves when the armored upper door was lowered.

Rear armor was bolted on and had a solid rear plate with no rear access. Tripods for the .50 caliber and .30 caliber machine guns were strapped to the rear plate, with a bumper or shelf below. A standard military taillight was on the left, and blackout lights were on the right. The standard military pintle hitch was

White M3A1 Scout Car
This view of Jack Terrill's scout car shows much about the vehicle. In the foreground, is the spring-mounted roller with tow hooks and cable, the early automotive-type headlights on the contoured front fenders, and the late-style combat wheels with 10-ply 8.25x20 tires. Storage and weapons show the .50 caliber and two .30 caliber machine guns on their pintle, cradle, and skate rail assemblies. Above the driver's door, the crash padding on the skate rail is in place. The pioneer tools and canvas water bucket are clearly visible. A rare 50-round ammunition can for the .50 caliber machine gun is also seen here. Jack Terrill

White M3A1 Scout Car
At the center of the vehicle, the battery box and ax with its leather storage strap are visible. The upper door armor is down in its stowed position. The radio antenna is center mounted and tied down to each rear corner of the body. Early in the war, the numbers on the side of the hood were painted light gray rather than white because in a black and white aerial reconnaissance photo the light gray could not be distinguished from the olive drab paint. Jack Terrill

in the rear for towing a trailer. A canvas top and bows were strapped on with footman loops.

The interior of the truck had a conventional automotive layout. The instrument panel used round civilian gauges, consisting of a speedometer with odometer in one cluster and a second cluster containing the fuel, amp, oil pressure, and temperature gauges. A voltmeter was used on occasion or installed when vehicles were rebuilt. An electric trailer brake control was mounted on the dash with choke and throttle cables. Many scout cars had heaters under the dash and a glovebox located on the right side. The main data plate was to the right of the glovebox door.

The steering column mounted a black plastic steering wheel with a horn button reading "Ross" for the steering gear manufacturer. A four-speed manual transmission with

a two-speed transfer case had floor-mounted levers. A disc-type parking brake was mounted on the rear of the transmission.

The rear interior of these trucks had six bucket-type seats with seat and backrest cushions. The radio antenna base was located in the center. An SCR506, 508, or 510 radio set was mounted just below it.

Around the top of the body and traveling completely around the interior was the skate rail for the machine gun mounts. Each mount sat on a trolley with a hand release so it could be moved around the entire vehicle. A .50 caliber machine gun with pintle, cradle, and skate was normally mounted at the front, with two water-cooled M1917A1 or air-cooled M1919A4 .30 caliber machine guns in the rear. A Thompson submachine gun was also provided. Approximately 8,000 rounds of .30 caliber ammunition, 750 rounds of .50

White M3A1 Scout Car
Detail of the footman loops to tie down the canvas top at the tank's rear. Bracketry, straps, and the two .30 caliber tripods are just above the rear storage plates. In the center is the large .50 caliber tripod. The pintle *hitch, rear bumper, taillight, and blackout marker lights are clearly visible. The two 1917A1 Browning .30 caliber replicas with their wooden ammunition boxes are a fine example of this vehicle's weaponry.*
Jack Terrill

caliber ammunition, and 540 rounds of ammunition for the .45 caliber Thompson were carried.

The powertrain of the scout car was standard truck design. A Hercules JXD six-cylinder gasoline engine was under the hood, cooled by a fin-and-tube radiator with a six-blade fan and an overflow tank. A Zenith Model 29 carburetor fed fuel to the engine; Donaldson provided an oil-bath air cleaner for the carburetor. Ignition came from a shielded, 12-volt system; Delco Remy of GM made the generator, voltage regulator, and

starter. The clutch was a single disc setup, coupled to a Spicer four-speed transmission with synchromesh in second, third, and fourth gear. The two-speed transfer case was mounted separately from the transmission and was unique because of its "full-time" four-wheel-drive. High and low range were provided with a ratio of 1.00:1 and 1.87:1.

The truck was propelled by Timken differential assemblies running on tapered roller bearings. The differentials were of split design, meaning that one half had to be unbolted from the spring to service the unit. The differential ratio was 5.14:1, which gave the truck a high top speed. Drum-type brakes were used with a power vacuum booster, which was mounted on the frame. Conventional leaf springs suspended the vehicle with the front springs on the top of the axle housing and the rear springs under the rear axle to lower the height in the rear. Early units used standard truck wheels with large vent holes; later models were equipped with combat wheels. The combat wheels had a bolt-on lock ring and a bead lock inside to keep the 12-ply nylon 8.25x20in tire from collapsing when shot out, providing enough support to get out of harm's way.

Top speed of the M3A1 was 60+mph. Fuel capacity was 30gal giving a range of approximately 250 miles. The fuel tank was located under the driver's seat.

The heavy weight of the M3A1 limited its off-road performance. Gross weight of the truck was 12,400lb combat loaded, and so the vehicle could climb a maximum grade of 60 percent, clear vertical obstacles of 12in, and ford depths of 28in. Angles of approach were 37deg in front and 35deg at the rear.

Length of the M3A1 was 18ft, 5 1/2in, width 6ft, 8in, and height 6ft, 6 1/2in. Ground clearance was 15 1/2in, tread center to center was 65 1/4in, wheelbase 131in, and ground pressure 60psi.

The scout car was used by armored units and cavalry divisions. It was primarily a hard-road vehicle because of its high ground pressure per square inch. As the war went on, improved cross-country mobility was a must

and the half-track was created. In the last part of the war, the armored units eventually wanted high-speed, full-tracked vehicles to keep up with the fast pace of the tanks themselves and so the M3A1 was retired from service.

After 1945, many scout cars were given away to developing nations under military aid packages and remained in service for decades after World War II conflicts had ended. It was a light, fast, economical vehicle that was quite easy to maintain. With its weapons systems, it could provide fast support when needed.

Scout cars were used more in the North African, Italian, and western European areas of combat in World War II. The jungles and rough terrain, combined with the lack of roads limited them somewhat in the Pacific theater of operations. The Marines were the first forces in the Pacific theater, and the scout car was really used more by the Army than the Marines.

M8 and M20 Armored Cars

The M8 and M20 armored cars were the United States' first vehicles of their type and signified a dramatic change from the scout car. Whereas the scout cars were basically armored trucks, the M8/M20 was a completely new design built with specific purposes and uses in mind.

The M8 was intended as a tank destroyer, but British intelligence soon reported that the 37mm M6 gun was ineffective for direct confrontation involving enemy armor. In a sense,

White M3A1 Scout Car
The Browning M2 heavy-barrel .50 caliber machine gun. The gun mounts in the cradle-and-pintle assembly, which in turn sits in the socket of the skate rail. A lever fastens the gun in the socket, and a handle moves the assembly from left or right around the entire inside of the vehicle. Supporting the rear of the gun is the T & E or traverse-and-elevation mechanism for fine adjustments. Below the gun mount is the steering wheel and its "Ross" horn button. Jack Terrill

the M8 was obsolete for its original purpose before it was built. But it turned out to be a popular—and fast—vehicle excellent for mobile armored reconnaissance, light defensive work, and fire support.

The all-new body of the M8 featured heavier armor than the M3A1 and was of one-piece welded construction. The chassis was a full six-wheel-drive unit.

The M8's armored hull was a one-piece unit jig-welded with stainless-steel rod. The powertrain was mounted directly to the body with a sheet-metal panel separating the engine compartment from the fighting compartment.

The outside body had fenders or sand shields front and rear. The rear shields were hinged and easily removed; these were not used in combat because they were so easily damaged and because they made tire chains difficult to put on. Storage boxes were mounted on the top of the rear fenders with lids and a plate for the radio antenna between the small front and rear storage boxes, which held tools and spare parts. On the sides of the vehicle were mine racks that held three mines each. Later models had additional storage boxes on the outside of the hull.

The outside of the body had lifting eyes on each corner, blackout drive headlights that

White M3A1 Scout Car
Looking down into the rear body of the scout car, we see the bucket seats with canvas covers. The radio and antenna mount are at the center. The diamond plate floor can be seen. The diamond pattern embossed in this metal is a smaller pattern than used today. Above each wheel well, a cabinet has been installed for general storage. A crew of eight with their gear in a scout car made extra room hard to come by. The skate rail goes around the entire interior, and all three guns can be put in any position enabling any crew member to fire them. Jack Terrill

were removable from their sockets, and a small siren on the front. A storage box was mounted on the front of the hull between the headlights. Small metal strips were welded on the front below the hatches to help deflect bullets.

The engine was accessed by two heavy lids in the rear with ventilation openings to let air pass down through the top of the engine compartment then out through the rear.

Armored louvers covered the radiator in the rear. Tow shackles were placed front and rear, with a special rear pintle hitch. A rope could be tied to this hitch and then released by the driver to drop a trailer. The M8 occasionally towed an M10 ammunition trailer or a one-ton cargo trailer.

With a whole new interior and power-train layout, the driver and assistant driver/radio operator sat in the front, each with top and front hatches. In the hatches were direct vision slots and protectoscopes, similar in function to a periscope but smaller in size. The vehicle's data plate was located between the driver and assistant driver's hatches.

The driver rode on the left side with a conventional steering column, wheel, and sector used to steer the unit. An instrument panel sat on top of the steering column with standard round military gauges. The transmission and transfer case controls were on his right, and conventional foot controls were on the floor at his feet. A unique feature of the rear-engined M8/M20 was the use of a hydraulic accelerator and clutch pedal. The braking system used a standard automotive master cylinder with a vacuum-assist hydrovac booster.

The front seats were a cushion on the floor with a padded, fold-down backrest. Early M8s and M20s did not have an armored floor and land mines were potentially deadly. Most were modified by adding armor plate to the floor covering the driver's seat and legs; later vehicles were built with an armored floor.

The assistant driver served as a radio man for the vehicle using an SCR506, 508, 510, 608, or 610 radio set. Four interphone stations were provided with interphones in the crew's helmets, which were modified leather football helmets of the period.

Storage compartments were built into the sponsons of the M8, on the sides between the front axle and the front rear axle. Ammunition racks were mounted on the left side and the radio was on the right side.

The turret was power or manually transversed. Although it did not have a basket, its seat assemblies moved with it. The turret itself was cast with an open top. A pedestal-type .50 caliber machine gun mount was at the rear of the turret above the pistol port. Later vehicles were fitted with the M49 ring mount on three legs above the turret. The 37mm M6 gun on its M23A1 mount had a cast mantlet and .30 caliber machine gun coaxilally mounted. Eighty rounds of 37mm ammunition were carried with 400 rounds for the .30 caliber carbine, 400 rounds for the .50 caliber, and 1,500 rounds for the .30 caliber machine gun.

The powertrain was at the rear of the vehicle. The 56gal fuel tank was between the engine and fighting compartment. Early units had a steel tank, later models had a rubber tank. The engine was a 320ci JXD L-head six-cylinder model. An oil-bath air cleaner and Zenith Model 29 downdraft carburetor were used. The battery was on the right side. At the rear were two belt-driven fans with a full-width radiator. Air diffusers were attached to the radiator for proper dispersal of air.

The transmission was behind a standard dry-disc clutch. The transmission was most unusual in that it was a truck unit with the shifting mechanism on the side and linkage going forward to the remote shifter. It also had synchromesh in all four forward gears. A two-speed transfer case took in power from the transmission and distributed it to the

Timken split-design axles, which had a ratio of 6.6:1. The axle housings were wider than truck models and had armored tubing. Double driveshafts went to the rear axles with a pillow block for the rear-most shaft. Leaf spring suspension was used front and rear. In the rear, it was inverted and walking with a Timken six-torque-rod setup.

The brakes had two cylinders per wheel with a hydrovac for additional stopping power. Combat wheels were 9.00x20in with 12-ply nylon tires. These wheels had an armored center, bolt-on lock ring, and bead lock so the tires wouldn't collapse when shot out. These features allowed the truck to get out of harm's way—at least for a short distance.

The M20 was a fully armored vehicle as well. When armor plate is sloped or at an angle, the thickness as well as the deflection of projectiles are both increased. The actual thickness of the M8/M20 armor was as follows: hull upper front: 5/8in; hull lower

Ford M20 Armored Car
Ralph Doubek's beautifully restored Ford M20 armored car, serial number 2704, sits on display at the Iola Military Show in Iola, Wisconsin. The unique design and body are clearly evident here. Driver and assistant sit right up front; the Hercules JXD engine sits at the rear. The M49 ring mount for the .50 caliber gun was new and different from the unit used in the scout car, which was smaller and circular. The rear sand shields and front fenders with the mine racks in between are nicely defined in this photo. The front hatches with their protectoscopes and the combat pedestal-type headlights cover the front of the vehicle. The sloped armor and one-piece welded body are quite a departure from earlier designs based on truck chassis.
Tom Berndt

Ford M20 Armored Car
The rear of the M20 shows its unique rear engine compartment. It was an incredibly quiet vehicle. Air for cooling the engine was drawn down under the domed lids on the top hatches; then, double belt-driven rear fans pushed it out the rear through the radiator. Shields down along the oil pan prevented dust and dirt

from being drawn from the bottom through the engine compartment. It had equal weight on all three axles, which made its full six-wheel-drive efficient and provided a comfortable ride for the crew of six. The dual radio antennas are mounted between the storage boxes on top of the rear sand shields. Tom Berndt

front: 3/4in; hull sides: 3/8in; rear: 3/8in; top: 1/4in; bottom: 1/8in to 1/4in; turret front: 3/4in; and turret sides and rear: 3/4in.

M8s and M20s were fast, quiet vehicles. With their engine at the rear, enclosed in armor, and the fans pushing the air rearward, they could hardly be heard other than up close. Top speed was 60mph with a 60 percent gradeability. Vertical obstacle ability was 12in with a 24in fording depth. The 56gal fuel

tank gave it a driving range of approximately 350 miles.

These vehicles were also compact, making them maneuverable. The vehicle was only 16ft, 5in long and 8ft, 4in wide. Its profile was also reasonably low at 7ft, 4 1/2in. Its short overall length—with a 128in wheelbase from center of the rear axles to the center of the front—made it hardly longer than a modern pickup truck. Ground pressure was about

M8 Armored Car

David Wright's M8 armored car is a later model of the production run. It has a different side storage cabinet in place of the small mine rack. The M8 and M20 chassis were nearly identical, but their center fighting compartments were different. The superstructure was replaced with a cast turret and a 37mm gun. The mount was a M23A1 with a .30 caliber coaxially mounted machine gun. Muzzle velocity of the 37mm gun was 2,900ft per second, penetrating 1.8in of face-hardened armor plate at 1,000yd. The commander and gunner sat in seats that rotated with the manually traversed turret. The gunner used an M70D telescopic sight. Ammunition used was M51B1 or M51B2 armor piercing, M63 high explosive, or M2 canister. Eighty rounds were carried on the vehicle. Ford Motor Company built all the M8s and M20s. M8s were built first, and the M20s were standardized later. Approximately 8,700 M8s and 3,700 M20s were built.
Tom Berndt

13.6psi at 3in penetration. One interesting fact is that the M8s and M20s had almost equal weight on each axle, giving them a good ride and excellent traction.

The M20 had a small superstructure welded in place of the M8's turret. An M49 circular ring mount, carrying a skate with a pintle-mounted .50 caliber machine gun, was mounted on three legs above the superstructure. The interior had two wooden bench seats and a single rear seat for the crew. Radios were carried in the right sponson; a map table was at the front of the superstructure for the commander. Racks for the .30 caliber carbines were in the right rear corner. Vehicle ammunition storage was located in the left sponson on the M8.

2

Half-Tracks

The Army's upgrading of its equipment in the late 1930s reflected the need for increased cross-country mobility. Half-tracks were considered in the mid-1930s based on converted civilian trucks.

The White Motor Company was a natural selection for the construction of the half-track. After successfully building the scout car, White used its shape and form in the design of the half-track. Although similar in appearance, the scout car and half-track were completely different vehicles and virtually no parts interchanged.

Half-tracks were used mainly in armored divisions as transports for infantry in support of tank columns. Several basic types were used—principally by the Army and Marine Corps—in the European and Pacific theaters of war. Basically there were four different uses: personnel carriers, mortar carriers, antiaircraft gun mounts, and gun motor carriages for larger guns.

Many experimental models of half-tracks, as well as numerous production models, were built. Completely new, more-sophisticated chassis were designed, including newly designed components of the vehicles.

As time went on during the war, White's half-track production capacity was not adequate and Autocar Truck Company and Diamond T Truck Company were needed to assist. The vehicles produced by these three companies were identical in every way.

Even with this additional capacity, more were needed; International Harvester Company got into the picture and built several models on a similar chassis. IHC, in fact, used some of the components White used, but also had major differences in the body and power-

M2A1 Half-Track
The track itself was two long cables coiled with crossbars clamped over it, one on each side. A center guide was bolted in the middle. Each cable was on one side of the center guide. Rubber was vulcanized onto this, under heat, on a hot flat press, thus making an endless rubber surface for the rubber-tired bogie wheels to run on. Track life was said to be about 1,000 miles.
Tom Berndt

White M4A1 Mortar Carrier
This White M4A1 mortar carrier was one of the earlier designs of the half-track, and belongs to David Wright. Here we see the shorter body, which was also used on the M2 personnel carrier, along with short mine racks and side storage compartments with exterior doors.

Additional storage cabinets sat at the rear of the body. The front half of this M4A1 is similar to the scout car; even the same type of skate rail was used, but they were completely different vehicles. The Tulsa 18G 10,000lb winch at the front adds more length to the unit. Note the later pedestal headlights. Tom Berndt

train components. All of the different items used by International Harvester were not interchangeable with the White.

All the Whites had the same basic chassis, powertrain, and front armor; the differences were mainly in the rear body. The IHC units were also done in the same manner, with rear body configurations as the main differences.

M2, M3, M4, M5, M9, and M21 Half-Tracks

The M2 half-track was the first to be built, as early as 1940. This vehicle had a shorter body with no rear door in the armor. It had seats for ten crew members with a skate rail that surrounded the interior of the vehicle. It carried two, or sometimes three, carriage mounts for a .50 caliber and one or two .30 caliber air- or water-cooled machine guns. It had short mine racks on the side toward the rear and exterior doors for storage compartments on each side just behind the front doors. The M2 was equipped with a front-mounted roller or power-take-off-driven winch with a 10,000lb capacity.

The M2A1 was the same basic vehicle as the M2, but the skate rail and carriages were substituted for a circular M49 ring mount about the front passenger's seat on the right side of the vehicle. Three fixed pintle sockets were positioned on the body, one on each side and one at the rear.

The M3 configuration had quite a few improvements over the M2 units. The rear body was lengthened to the end of the frame, and a rear door was added. Thirteen seats were provided for troops, three across the front and five down each side in the rear. An M25 pedestal mount for a .50 caliber machine gun was mounted just behind the center front seat. The two 30gal fuel tanks were located in the rear of the body on each side behind the seats.

The M3A1 had the pedestal mount eliminated and the M49 ring mount installed along with the three pintle sockets on the sides and rear of the body. The M3A2 was a slightly modified M3A1 with rear exterior fold-down storage racks on each side of the rear door.

Full-length mine racks were on the sides of all M3s. The interior storage was rearranged to accommodate five to twelve crew members. The fuel tanks were moved for-

M4A1 Half-Track
Fred Ropkey's M4A1 half-track displays the front spring-mounted roller and earlier automotive-type headlights. Ammunition was carried in the side cabinet. This vehicle had the early small idler spring *for the real idler wheel. The .50 caliber machine gun and mount used in the M2 and M4 series half-tracks would interchange with the ones used in the scout cars.* Tom Berndt

ward to just behind the driver and passenger seats. If radios were carried, seats were usually displaced, or if the vehicles were used as machine gun squad carriers, fewer crew were carried. Anywhere from 2,000 to 7,000 rounds of .30 caliber ammunition were carried, depending on the model.

The body configurations of the IHC half-tracks coincided with the Whites. The M5 had the same seating arrangement and pedestal mount as the M3. The M5A1 was also the same as the M3A1, with the M49 mount and sockets. The M9A1 was similar to the M2A1 with seating for ten and storage and radio

M4A1 Half-Track
The M4A1 half-track rear compartment. The M4A1 had a small rear door installed in the rear armor. The 81mm mortar was installed to be fired from the vehicle. The metal plates behind the armor plate are seen behind the skate rail. The fuel tank is a rubber-coated metal tank, which hinders sparks if the tank is punctured. A thin metal shield covers it, and the backrests of the seat attach to it. These tanks were the same in almost all the half-tracks. Cardboard canisters held the mortar rounds. The mortar base was fastened to the vehicle's frame with a rubber shock mount for cushioning. Tom Berndt

Autocar M3A1
George Hilton's 1941 Autocar M3A1, serial number 560, soaks up the late November sun. "Darin" received a total restoration and overhaul of all components. The 2nd Armored Division markings set off this fine vehicle. The large circle around the hood star nearly covers the width of both lids.
George Hilton

cabinets behind the driver and passenger, but this vehicle again had the M49 ring mounts and sockets. Exterior side doors were not used on the International Harvester models.

The early M4 performed the role of a mortar carrier. The vehicle carried ammunition, crew, and an 81mm mortar that could be fired from the vehicle in an emergency. It had the same body configuration as the M2 personnel carrier with a rear door added; the skate rail around the interior was used in this unit as well.

The M4A1 was modified so the 81mm mortar was fixed in the vehicle and fired toward the rear. Each unit had a crew of six. The M4A1 had storage boxes on the back of the hull as well as next to the rear door. Again, the skate rail weapons mount was used.

The final version was the M21 mortar carrier based on the longer-bodied M3 half-track with the mortar mounting reversed to fire toward the front. Ammunition was carried inside in racks, with the fuel tanks in the rear-most corners. At the rear center of the fighting compartment was a pedestal mount for a .50 caliber machine gun. Full-length mine racks were on the sides, with folding storage racks at the rear of the body. This unit had no rear door.

M3, M15, and M16 Motor Gun Carriages

There were many gun motor carriages, most of which were based on the M3 body and chassis. A large variety were built as prototypes, but only two were really used to any degree in combat. Some of the guns used were the 40mm Bofors; 57mm anti-tank gun; 75mm, called the "French 75"; the 105mm Howitzer; and many multiple-gun combinations. Two of the multiple-gun carriages were used for anti-aircraft defense with great success.

Only the 57mm and 75mm guns were used in combat to any large degree. Basically, they were mounted on their carriages on the

Autocar M3A1
An excellent view of the M3A1 shows good detail of the flat plate-armored body of the White, Autocar, and Diamond T half-track vehicles. The rear door, top bows, and mine racks are clearly seen here. The great majority of half-tracks found by collectors are missing their rear bodies; they were of little value to someone using the truck for commercial use and so were often removed. George Hilton

M3 Half-Track
The interior of Ralph Doubek's M3 half-track. Three men sat across the front and normally five on each side of the rear. One seat has been displaced for a radio set. The base of the M25 center pedestal mount is clearly seen. The canvas on the side of the mount covers lines

for a gas-firing replica .50 caliber machine gun. Fuel tanks can been seen at the forward part of the compartment. Storage compartments were under the floor in between the frame rails. Bottom seat cushions used a soldier's woolen blanket for padding. Tom Berndt

half-track's frame just behind the driver's compartment. The wheels were removed, the rails were shortened, and a new gun shield was fitted. The windshield folded down onto the cowl and interior storage was rearranged to suit the needs of the gun crew. After combat use in North Africa and other theaters, the armored vehicle commanders soon realized that the guns were not effective on the

rapidly improving enemy armor. Their uses changed and other weapons systems slowly replaced them, but they were used toward the end of the war in less active roles.

The multiple-gun carriages that were used in combat were the M15, M15A1, and the M16. These were used for armored column and general anti-aircraft defense. The M15 had a 37mm fully automatic cannon

M3 Half-Track
The half-track's front roller assembly. Brackets were riveted to the frame and held the tensioning springs in place. These units are frequently missing on vehicles found by collectors. Don Douda mounted his siren on the bumper and elected to paint his tow hooks yellow. Half-tracks had a horn under the hood, and tow hooks were painted the same color as the vehicle.
Tom Berndt

White M3 Half-Track
An excellent example of the Tulsa 18G winch on the front of Ralph Doubek's White half-track. This winch was used on all the half-tracks, both White and International Harvester Company models. The massive front bumper was riveted to the frame with extensions to provide room for the winch. After the war, the winch was rated at 25,000lb for civilian use. The armored radiator shutters and combat-type headlights are seen here. Tom Berndt

with two .50 caliber machine guns. Early models had an open platform with a manually operated gun mount; later ones had an armored enclosure around the mount. The M15A1 had a slightly different mount with rearrangements of the ammunition storage, seating, armor, and guns. These models proved effective in North Africa, and several hundred were built.

The M16 proved to be the final model, using a power-operated Maxson turret. A small gasoline-engine-driven generator was on the back of the mount and it would traverse a full 360deg very quickly. The floor of the half-track was raised so the mount could

clear the side armor, and the top 4in of side armor was hinged for additional clearance. It used four .50 caliber Browning machine guns, each firing 400–500 rounds per minute. Needless to say, it was a potent weapon system. A plane flying through a hail of fire produced by these guns would have a difficult time surviving if the gunner was good. The gunner sat in the center of the mount. A crew of five operated the unit. It was radio equipped, as was the M15 and M15A1. Interior storage was rearranged again for this particular use of the vehicle.

M16 Half-Track

Four Browning .50 caliber replicas pointed skyward on Jacques Littlefield's M16 quad mount. The front armor and sight for the gunner are shown along with the 200-round ammunition chests. Each gun could fire 600 rounds per minute. This was an effective weapons system. Traverse and elevation were extremely fast. The gunner sat in a cramped position in the center with his controls. The fold-down sides of the M16 are seen here. Tom Berndt

The half-track had a most distinctive appearance, and there has not been anything built quite like it since. It was a relatively simple vehicle whose design proved to be successful. The original vehicles had a single frame-rail construction, but a weak point right above the rear axle housing was soon discovered. Here the frame curved upward to go over the rear axle housing and had a tendency to crack. Shortly thereafter, this construction was replaced with a full double-frame rail on each side.

The chassis was a basic truck unit with some slight design changes for the rear axle and suspension. At the front was either a roller for undiching itself or a power takeoff-driven winch. A conventional split-housing front-drive axle by Timken was mounted on conventional leaf springs. Manual steering gear built by Ross was used. A White 160AX

M16 Half-Track
This M16 has the fold-down armor, which gave it a lower profile. The M16A1s used in Korea were usually rebuilt M3 series or M15 series units and did not have the fold-down armor. They had a much taller profile and used the darker paint of the Korean era and M

series vehicles. "Chatterbox" is an appropriate name for an M16. At the rear, the M16 had no door for access. The fuel tanks were moved forward, right behind the driver and commander's seats. The radio set is seen behind the commander's position. Tom Berndt

L-head 386ci engine with 128hp net and 300lb-ft of torque at 1200rpm moved the vehicle at speeds up to 40–45mph. The vehicles weighed about 15,000–20,000lb, depending on the model.

A four-speed manual transmission with an attached two-speed transfer case gave ample gear reduction. The rear axle was bolted solid to the frame and was a banjo type. Drive sprockets replaced wheels and engaged the endless band track. The track had rubber vulcanized over a set of steel cables with cross bars for reinforcements. Center guides kept the track in place. A Kegresse-type suspension system with four pairs of bogie tires was used. A top support roller and a spring-

tensioned idler at the rear kept the track tight. At the rear were two bumperettes and a pintle hitch.

The half-track's body and armor were built of face-hardened 1/4in armor plate. The flat plate was bolted together or onto a framework of steel reinforcements. The windshield was hinged, folding up with direct vision slots. At the front, a set of armored louvers covered the radiator. These louvers were operated by a lever near the front passenger's right foot, enabling him to open or close them when needed. The front fenders were heavy steel, and early half-tracks had truck-type headlights with heavy wire screen in front of them for protection; later models had what

M16 Half-Track
The rear of the quad mount had the gasoline-engine-driven generator mounted on it. The gunner entered the turret just above it. The four guns would normally have had an electric firing solenoid on the back of each receiver. It was a Maxson-type turret and was a Model 45D. It was developed by the W. L. Maxson Company. The later M45F mount used on the M16A1s had large armored shields, often referred to as "batwing" armor. Tom Berndt

M16 Half-Track
On its way out to the field, the M16 shows its compact silhouette. Tom Berndt

were called a pedestal type. This light sat in a socket and was removable when not needed. A steel plug was used to insert in the socket when the lights were stored. Fittings on the sides of the body under the doors held the pioneer tools: ax, shovel, and pick ax.

At the rear of the body was a door for rear access. The floor of the vehicle was not armored and was built out of diamond plate. Storage compartments were built into the floor above the rear suspension. Fuel tanks were placed along the sides behind the seats and were rubber covered for fire protection when penetrated. Rifle racks and storage

were also behind the seats. The fuel tanks were usually mounted just behind the driver and assistant or at the rear corners of the body, depending on the model.

The driver's compartment had standard truck-type controls and instruments. A left and right seat were used; sometimes a third center seat was installed, depending on the model.

The half-track was a rugged, simple vehicle whose design was most enduring. France produced International Harvester models under license for some years after World War II. Israel modified several thousand units for its armed forces and used them for years after the country's independence. Israel still uses them today, but most have been repowered with diesel engines. Approximately 21,000 half-tracks were built in World War II by all manufacturers.

M16 Half-Track
Jacques Littlefield's M16 half-track. A crew of five serviced the vehicle: a commander, gunner, two loaders, and the driver. The guns had an interrupter feature so they wouldn't fire when going over the driver's compartment. The control grips are mounted on a post between the gunner's knees. Handlebar rotation on a vertical plane controls the turret traverse. There was an earlier half-track, the M13, which had a power turret, but used only two .50 caliber machine guns. Tom Berndt

M16 Half-Track
The rear stowage cabinets are clearly seen in this bright, sunlit photo. The dark, rich color of the M series paint is evident here. Tom Berndt

M16 Half-Track
Ralph Doubek's M16 at the Iola Military Show, backed by a GMC CCKW dump truck. The center of the mount had two small shields that folded up, one on each side of the gunner's sights. The side armor is in its travel position, and the base of the mount is almost even with the top of the body. The turret could be elevated from -10deg to +90deg, and has a traverse of 360deg, with maximum speed of traverse at 60deg per second. Tom Berndt

M2A1 Half-Track
Here is a fine example of an M2A1, owned by Jacques Littlefield. A completely restored unit, the A1 designation shows the M49 ring mount installed on an M2 vehicle. Additional storage racks and three pintle sockets were put on the rear of the body. The skate rail was removed when the vehicle was reconditioned by the Army. Tom Berndt

38

M2A1 Half-Track
The rear storage racks added with the M2's A1 designation were large. Here we can see examples of the small mines used in the racks. These particular ones are practice or dummy units and are a rare accessory and difficult to find. A .30 caliber air-cooled Browning replica sits in the rear socket mount. Tom Berndt

Previous page
M2A1 Half-Track
The M2A1 is nicely silhouetted against the skyline here showing the machine guns and mounts. The radio antenna used several sections and was quite tall. Fourth armored division markings have been assigned to this truck. Tom Berndt

M2A1 Half-Track
The half-track's rear suspension and track assembly were most unique. It used a Kegresse-type suspension with two vertical volute springs and a series of two bogie clusters per side with four wheels per cluster. The bogie wheels needed constant lubrication because they were not completely sealed. A great deal of grease would get past the seals when they got hot. George Hilton

M9A1 Half-Track

Andre Gibeau's M9A1 sits fully equipped with all its gear and Canadian markings. Most International Harvester half-tracks went to Lend-Lease countries. England, France, and Russia all received them. There were many differences: radiator, engine, differentials, and the entire body were some of the major items. Tracks and suspension were interchangeable. From a distance, the front fenders were the most noticeable as well as the rounded rear corners of the one-piece rear armor. George Hilton

M9A1 Half-Track

The M9A1's full canvas was a beautiful piece of workmanship, with leather corner reinforcements, brass zippers, and grommets. The large rear stowage racks were added to later-production half-tracks. The Canadian markings were quite different than United State's ones in size, shape, and sometimes color.
George Hilton

3

Light Tanks

The light tanks used by the United States in World War II had their origins in the T5, M1, and M2 series of light tanks from the late 1930s. The first T5 was built in 1934, and M2s were built as late as 1941. These tanks led to the development of the M3 series used early in the war and the M5 series as the last of the original light tanks.

Numerous prototypes of light tanks and gun carriages were built during the 1941–1945 period. The experiences of the M3 and M5, along with the enemy's armor designs, led to the need for better units for the United States.

The two most prominent models were the M18 Hellcat Tank Destroyer and the M24

Chaffee light tank. These were built in quantity and had the best improvements based on experience in actual combat.

All four of these vehicles were used in the European and Pacific theaters of war. Many were given away as Lend-Lease or foreign aid during the war. After World War II, many of the models were used for years by Third World countries. The M24 Chaffee even underwent a repower program, which added diesel engines and up-to-date automatic transmissions.

M3 Light Tank

M3 tank production began in March 1941 at American Car and Foundry. In 1941 and 1942, 4,526 were built with the Continental W-670 gasoline radial aircraft engine, and 1,285 M3s were built with a Guiberson radial diesel engine. About 3,200 of this group were given away under foreign aid.

The M3 tank turret had a power traverse mechanism and gyro stabilizer added to the turret and gun. This necessitated a turret bas-

M5A1 Light Tank
This overall view shows the top of the vehicle. The larger double hatches on the top of the turret are open. The tow cable stretches the length of the vehicle. Grouser bars are bolted to the side of the turret for added armor protection. The front hatches show the M6 periscopes and their mounts. Note the rubber tired rear idler wheel. At the rear of the vehicle is the large stowage box for tools and equipment. Tom Berndt

M3A1 Light Tank

Entrance and exit of the driver of Frank Buck's M3 series tank, serial number 10197, was strenuous to say the least. He had one hatch that folded up and another above his legs that went forward. The assistant driver had an even more difficult time with only one hatch in front of him. This photo shows the flat, vertical plate of the hull and turret, giving almost no slope to the armor at all. The turret was welded with a cast mantlet and 37mm M5 or M6 and mounted in an M22, M23, or M44 mount. A total of 116 rounds of ammunition were carried for the main gun. American Car and Foundry manufactured this unit.

Tom Berndt

M3A1 Light Tank

The Continental seven-cylinder radial engine was at the rear of the M3 series. As you can see, the air cleaners were mounted externally. The aircraft type engines used in the tanks were compact and powerful and were ideal for the vehicles. The suspension of these vehicles was much different than the torsion bar used later. It worked well. Note the large trailing idler at the rear. This is a later M3A1 with a welded hull; M3s had riveted hulls. Tom Berndt

ket with seats because the crew could not turn quickly enough with this new equipment. This became the M3A1, with other small improvements added as well. Production started in May 1942 and ended in February 1943; it became obsolete in July 1943. Most of the 4,621 M3A1s built had the W670 Continental radial gas engine; a small quantity had the Guiberson diesel radial engine.

The hull and turrets of the M3 and M3A1 had an evolution of their own. The M3 originally had a riveted hull and turret. The next improvement was a rolled and welded turret and a riveted hull. The last improvement was a welded hull with a welded turret. Early turrets had a cupola and pistol ports.

The M3 series hull and turret were quite boxy and flat. Armor thickness in front was 1 1/2in; sides were 1in; and the top and bottom were 3/8in to 1/2in. The turret armor was 1 1/2in in front, 1 1/4in on the sides, and 1/2in on top. Overall weight was about 27,400lb gross for the M3 and 28,500lb for the M3A1.

As usual, the design was much the same as earlier tanks. The radial engine was at the

M5A1 Light Tank
Heading back to the barn, Jacques Littlefield's gorgeous M5A1 returns to the shop. The late afternoon sun shows much of the detail of the tank. The shield on the right side of the turret is for the anti-aircraft machine gun mount. At the rear is the raised deck for the Cadillac engine's radiators. These sat above the engines in a horizontal position. The intermittent bar cleat-type track is on this tank with the late solid bogie tires and wheels. Tom Berndt

rear with the driveshaft under the turret basket. Between the driver and the assistant was a five-speed, manual synchromesh transmission with overdrive, which was bolted directly to the mechanically controlled differential. Steering was accomplished by two levers used to brake oil-bathed bands inside the differential. Planetary final drives gave the drive sprockets additional gear reduction.

The driver and assistant sat in front. Each had a vertical hatch in front of them for entrance and exit; the driver had an additional hatch above his legs. The assistant driver did not have this because the bow-mounted .30 caliber machine gun was in front of him. The instrument panel sat on top of the transmission. An auxiliary generator sat on the bottom of the hull beneath the turret basket. A steel bulkhead separated the engine compartment from the fighting compartment.

The W-670 Continental radial engine sat at the rear with a pair of rear access doors for service. Pioneer tools were stowed on the rear of the tank. The air cleaners were mounted on the fenders above the rear idler wheels. Fuel tanks holding 54gal sat near the bulkhead just below the rear of the turret.

The Continental engine was a seven-cylinder radial with 668ci and 250hp. A hefty 584lb-ft of torque came at 1800rpm. It was air cooled, with a carburetor and 12-volt magneto-type ignition.

Guiberson built the diesel radial, a nine-cylinder model T-1020-4. Displacement was

1021ci, giving 220hp and 580lb-ft of torque at 1400rpm. The diesel-engined M3 and M3A1 vehicles were not used in combat by the United States. They used a most unusual starter that employed a shotgun-type cartridge similar to those used in some aircraft. The diesel engine was also somewhat problematic in cold weather.

The interior of the M3 tanks had fixed fire extinguisher systems. Radios were mounted in the left sponson, usually an SCR508 with four interphone stations for the crew of four.

The main armament of the M3 series was a 37mm M6 gun with a coaxial .30 caliber machine gun. A .30 caliber anti-aircraft gun was carried on the outside rear of the turret. Over 7,000 rounds of .30 caliber ammunition were carried, along with approximately 100 rounds for the main gun.

Tracks for the M3 series were 11 1/2in wide, double pin; several types were used, including smooth rubber block, rubber chevron, steel chevron, or steel parallel grouser. Two bogie clusters with vertical volute spring suspension and two bogie wheels per cluster gave the small tank a fairly good ride. A trailing rear idler was adjustable to keep the track tight.

With a total length of only 178in, the M3 series tanks were fast and maneuverable. Top

M5A1 Light Tank
The radical design change of the M5A1's front hull over the M3A1 is clearly seen here. It is well sloped with top hatches for the driver and assistant. The

M5A1's turret was enlarged at the rear for the radios, and much larger hatches were installed for the commander and gunner. Tom Berndt

M5A1 Light Tank
Frank Buck's "Ain't Walkin!" at the Redball Express Rally in Pennsylvania. Better detail of the rear bustle box is shown here. Spare track blocks and track jacks are at the rear corners of the hull. Three different types of bogie wheels are shown here: early spoked, welded spoked, and later stamped solid. Even the idler spokes have been welded shut. The radio antenna is at the rear of the turret. "Ain't Walkin!" was a Cadillac unit, serial number 4271. Tom Berndt

speed was 36mph and the cruising range was about 135 miles if the two additional 25gal fuel tanks were used.

The M3 tanks were well liked, but became obsolete in mid-war.

M5 Light Tank

The M5 series was a dramatic change for the light tanks due to its powertrain: the engines were still rear mounted, but now were liquid cooled.

The hull of the M5 series was enlarged. Longer, smoother sides, a better sloped front with easier access top hatches, and better vi-

sion for the driver and assistant headed the list of improvements. The rear deck was raised for the radiators that sat above each engine. Rear access doors were still retained. Fuel tanks were relocated to the rear corners of the hull. The M3A1 turret was used on the M5; the M5A1 had a much-improved and larger turret with a radio mount inside the rear of the turret. Tracks and suspension were nearly the same. The air cleaners were now concealed under the rear overhang by the rear access doors.

The M5 tanks came off the line in April 1942 and ended in December 1942 with a total production of 2,074 vehicles. The Cadil-

M24 Chaffee Light Tank
The M24's suspension was a great advance over the vertical volute springs used on the M3s and M5s. The torsion-bar setup rode much smoother and had better ground clearance. The shock absorbers here are mounted on the front two and rear two sets of road wheels. The front differential mounting was last used in this tank. All other new tanks designed after World War II used the new cross-drive transmission differential assembly, which was compact and mounted at the rear. This fine example belongs to David Wright's Wright Military Museum. Tom Berndt

lac Division of General Motors and Massey Harris built them at three different plants.

Engines were the big improvement in the M5 tanks. Radial engines were needed for aircraft production and alternatives were sought for the tanks. Cadillac installed two of its L-head 346ci automotive V-8s—each with its own Hydramatic transmission—in an M3A1 prototype. These were excellent, well-proven units. Two driveshafts then went forward to a two-speed synchronizing transfer unit bolted directly to the front differential. It was the same basic unit as the M3 differentials, but now it had dual driving controls mounted on the roof for the driver and assistant.

The M5A1 had the improved turret with additional room in the rear of it for the radios and an escape hatch in the floor behind the co-driver. A new mount for the .30 caliber anti-aircraft gun was placed on the side of the M5A1 turret. Later models had a shield over this unit. Much larger hatches were built into the top of the turret.

The M5A1 was quite a bit heavier than the early M3. With a little heavier armor and fully equipped, they were about 34,700lb.

M24 Chaffee Light Tank
This right front three-quarters view shows much of the detail of the M24. A more sleek and modern vehicle than the M3s and M5s, it was a great improvement over the other earlier light tanks. Above the front *access plate is the ventilator for the interior. The 75mm M6 gun sits in its cast mantlet and M64 mount. Forty-eight rounds of 75mm ammunition were carried. Note the spotlight on top of the turret. The turret was a one-piece casting as well.* Tom Berndt

Performance was about the same as the M3 with a top speed of 36mph.

M5A1s began production in November 1942. Some 6,810 units were built by Cadillac, Massey Harris, and American Car and Foundry until June 1944. M5A1 models were used as front-line equipment right up to the end of the war.

M24 Chaffee Light Tank

The M24 Chaffee was the final light tank built by the United States in World War II. The light tanks needed a larger gun; an at-tempt was made to modify an M5A1 with a 75mm gun, but it did not meet the require-ments as the turret was too small.

In March 1943, the designs of the M24 were set in motion. In late 1943, the first pilot vehicles were sent to Aberdeen Proving Grounds for tests. Cadillac and Massey Har-ris began production in April and July 1944. Manufacture of this model ceased at the end of the war in 1945. The two companies built 4,731 M24s.

The twin Cadillac V-8s in the M5A1s were well liked and dependable; when the M24 was designed, this powertrain was used on specific request. Consequently, a whole new vehicle was designed around it. The engines remained at the rear of the vehicle, but the 24-volt generators were mounted on the front of the engine block with a driveshaft under the intake manifold. The shaft ran the radiator fan. The radiator was mounted at an angle on top of the transmission near the distributor. Air was drawn in through the fighting compartment and exterior grates, then exhausted out the rear of the vehicle.

The engines were tied together with a two-speed transfer case located on the floor under the rear of the turret. From here a driveshaft went forward to the controlled differential at the front of the tank. The propeller shaft was a two-piece unit that ran through the wet stowage ammunition box arrangement on the floor of the vehicle. The left side of the shaft had four bins and the right side had three, leaving room for the hull floor escape hatch.

The driver and assistant sat in front on each side of the differential with dual driving controls. The assistant driver operated a .30 caliber machine gun in a ball socket-type bow mount. A large access plate was on the hull front for access to service or replace the differential.

The hull of the Chaffee was of all-welded plate. Thicknesses were 1in for front and sides, 3/4in for the rear, and 1/2in for the top and floor. Turrets had 1 1/2in fronts and 1in sides. All steel was rolled homogeneous plate. The angles of the hull were drastically

M24 Chaffee Ad
Cadillac supplied its engine and Hydramatic automatic transmission to the M24.

different than the M5 series; the M24s had a much better slope to the armor for greater deflection.

The hull rode on five dual-tired sets of road wheels per side, with torsion bar suspension. Drive sprockets were situated at the front and the adjusting idler at the rear. Tracks were single-pin steel with a 16in-wide center guide.

The turret held the 75mm main gun with a coaxial .30 caliber machine gun. The SCR508, 528, or 538 radio set was mounted in

M24 Chaffee Light Tank
The twin Cadillac V-8s sat at the rear of the tank. On the rear deck are the intake and exhaust grills, fuel tank covers, and radiator covers. From this view, you can see how short the M24 really is. The overall length of the hull is only 16ft, 3in. Gross weight was about 39,000lbs. *It was quite a substantial vehicle for a light tank. The rear of the turret shows the bustle with the radio inside behind the main gun. A gun mount sits on top for its .50 caliber machine gun, and a bustle storage box is at the very rear of the turret.*
Tom Berndt

the rear of the turret bustle. A gyrostabilizer was used with the power-operated turret. Forty-eight rounds of main gun ammunition were carried, with about 4,200 rounds of .30 and .50 caliber machine gun ammunition. Four .30 caliber submachine guns were car- ried for the crew, plus an exterior .50 caliber anti-aircraft machine gun on the top rear of the turret. The commander had a cupola and hatch with vision blocks on the left side of the turret, and the gunner had a large hatch on the right.

The dual 346ci Cadillac V-8s produced 220hp net and 488lb-ft of torque at 1200rpm. This combination with the extra gear reduction in the two-speed transfer case propelled the 38,000lb tank to 35mph. The 110gal fuel capacity gave it a range of 100–175 miles, depending on the terrain.

M19A1 Gun Carriage

A companion vehicle to the M24 Chaffee tank was the M19A1 twin 40mm anti-aircraft gun carriage. It was a redesigned M24 chassis with the entire engine compartment and its components moved forward to the center of the vehicle, just behind the driver and his as-

M24 *Chaffee* Light Tank
The M24 Chaffee was made up of flat plate and some castings. Here the bow mount for the assistant driver's .30 caliber machine gun is shown. In the center is the access cover for the controlled differential. At the top of the photo is the hatch for the assistant driver. Their

function had been somewhat redesigned on this tank. When initially opened, the lid went up a small amount and then swung out the side. This design allowed the hatch to open no matter what the turret position was.
Tom Berndt

M24 Chaffee Light Tank
Joe McClain's M24 Chaffee "Crusher." Here we see the commander's cupola a little better. The oversized siren is for parade use. The rubber chevron track was a second design. The earlier vehicles used an all-steel shoe track. These are nearly impossible to find today, and the rubber track is more conducive to use on asphalt streets. On a hot day, steel track will peel asphalt like butter and will windrow it in a turn.
Tom Berndt

sistant. The assistant had a radio mounted on his side, and the bow-mount machine gun was eliminated. The armor in the hull was thinner all around; most of the vehicle was made of 1/2in armor plate. Nearly all the powertrain, suspension, and other components were interchangeable with the M24 chassis.

At the rear of the M19A1 sat a large turret surrounded by ammunition boxes. In the center were fully automatic dual 40mm Bofors anti-aircraft guns. The turret had manual or hydraulic power traverse. A crew of six operated the vehicle. The guns were capable of 240 rounds per minute in short bursts. The vehicle carried about 350 rounds of 40mm ammunition. Gross weight was about 41,000lb, slightly heavier than the M24.

M19A1 gun carriages were built late in the war, in spring 1945. About 300 were built, none of which saw combat in World War II; however, they were used extensively in the Korean War several years later. Quite a few are still in collectors' hands today, popular because of the size and unique gun mount.

M18/M39 Hellcat Tank Destroyers

The M18 Hellcat is a fully tracked gun motor carriage, whose principal armament is the M1A1 76mm gun. It was an advanced vehicle at the date of its introduction in World War II and many of its characteristics were adopted in later vehicle designs. Speed was its best attribute: it is one of the fastest tracked, production-built vehicles ever manufactured for combat use. It will do in excess of 55mph sustained speed due to its light weight of approximately 39,000lb, combat loaded.

The hull was a solid, one-piece unit made up of individual armor plates welded together. The driver's compartment was in the front, the fighting compartment in the center, and the powerplant in the rear compartment.

M24/T24 Chaffee Light Tank
The darker paint color of this Chaffee was for the Korean era. The commander's hatch we see here was *similar to the one used on the late Sherman tanks. This is an early vehicle, serial number 21, built by Cadillac. The model was actually a T24.* Tom Berndt

The driver's compartment had two seating positions with the driver on the left and his assistant on the right. This vehicle had dual driving controls on each side. The steering levers were mounted on the roof of the compartment. The instrument panel was located in the left sponson. The Torqmatic automatic transmission with a shift selector mounted on it sat between the driver and assistant. The transmission was bolted directly to the controlled differential.

At the front of the vehicle was an access plate. When the bolts were removed, the plate could be laid down and fastened in place with support rods. On the back side of the plate were rails. The entire transmission-differential assembly could be slid out, set on the rails, and serviced. A hatch was provided for both driver and assistant and each had his own M6 periscope. A center-mounted siren was on the front hull above the access plate with the standard removable headlight as-

M19A1 Gun Carriage
A fine example of the M19A1 twin 40mm gun motor carriage owned by George DeBonis. This was a redesigned M24 hull with the engine compartment moved to the center of the chassis. The front compartment was the same and all chassis and powertrain components were the same. A large power-operated turret was added to the rear with two Bofors fully automatic 40mm guns. The guns were capable of 240 rounds per minute. They were hard load with clips of eight shells, fed from the top. The hull itself was made of thinner armor than the M24. The vehicle was originally intended for anti-aircraft defense of armored columns. It was supposed to have replaced the M15A1 half-track with its 37mm and twin .50 caliber machine guns. Tom Berndt

M19A1 Gun Carriage
Numerous ammunition cabinets surrounded the turret of the M19A1, which carried 336 rounds of 40mm ammunition. The doors under the rear of the turret were for a large storage area. The turret could traverse at 40deg per second. Muzzle velocity was 2,870ft per second. Note the large generator on the right fender— an improvement on the A1 designation of the M19. Tom Berndt

semblies and bush guards. The hull armor in front, sides, and rear was 1/2in.; top and bottom armor was 5/16in. This thin armor made the M18 lightweight, giving it its tremendous speed.

The turret on the M18 was a welded unit, mounting the 76mm main gun. The mount did not have a coaxially mounted machine gun. At the left rear of the open top turret was a circular ring mount for the .50 caliber machine gun. The main gun ammunition was carried in the turret and the floor. Forty-five rounds were carried. Five .30 caliber carbines, along with grenades, were carried for the five crew members. The gunner had hydraulic power or manual control of the turret. The gunner and commander were on the left side and the loader on the right. A partial turret basket moved with the turret. The rear turret bustle housed the radios, an SCR610 or British #19 set, with interphones and stations. The turret armor was thicker, with the front

M18 Hellcat Tank Destroyer
One of the rarest tracked vehicles in the world, this M18 "Hellcat" tank destroyer now belongs to the Military Museum of Southern New England. Robert Wichmann, their tracked vehicle coordinator, was kind enough to drive the vehicle out of storage and let me photograph it. It was truly a magnificent machine and in absolutely fantastic condition. The unit is nearly 100 percent complete. It was built by Buick, and only
a few thousand were manufactured. It was lightly armored, with a high horsepower-to-weight ratio. Consequently, it had tremendous speed. It would do in excess of 50mph on good roads. For an American tank, it used a most unusual track. All-steel shoe with rubber-bushed single pins and a drive sprocket with every other tooth engaging the track pins. The unique front access door for rolling out the differential is seen here. Tom Berndt

M18 Hellcat Ad
Buick built M18s for the Army and reminded

Americans on the home front of the firm's fine war materiel contribution.

and gun shield 3/4in to 1in thick and the sides and rear 1/2in thick. The turret exterior had provisions for storage of several types. Spare track shoes were normally carried at the rear.

In the interior, an oil cooler was used to cool transmission oil. This piece of equipment was converted in winter to provide heat for the crew, interior batteries, and engine compartment.

The engine was located at the rear of the hull, and like the transmission and differential in front, it also had a large rear access door that folded down, was supported, and provided a place for the entire engine to be

rolled out and serviced. It was a nine-cylinder, Continental radial aircraft engine, modified for ground use. Early vehicles had a C-1 model, which put out 400hp. Later vehicles had a C-4, which put out 450hp. The extra power came from a fixed-type supercharger that was added to the engine.

The radial engine was literally a round motor. The starter, magneto, and carburetor were at the rear in the center of the engine. It was air cooled by a fan attached to the flywheel, clutch, and pressure plate. A shroud surrounded the finned cylinders and heads; the fan drawing air through the finned cylinders cooled the engine. A dry-sump oiling system was used. Since the carburetor had no choke, a manual pumping system was used to inject fuel directly into the engine cylinders.

The engine had to be turned over by means of a hand crank; it took about fifty revolutions to clear the bottom cylinders of oil after the engine had set for some hours. Otherwise it could fire on the next piston past the bottom one, come around and blow the bottom engine cylinder off, being full of oil. A stainless-steel exhaust system with mufflers was used on this vehicle. Fuel tanks were on the left and at the sides of the engine, with filter caps on the top rear of the engine deck. Pioneer tools and a pintle hitch were on the rear of the hull.

For clearance purposes, the center of the engine crankshaft was quite high off the floor of the vehicle. A transfer case was used to direct the power down and forward through a driveshaft to the differential in front. A second transfer case directed the power up to the Torqmatic transmission in the front. Going through the transmission and differential, a driveshaft with U-joints sent the power to the final drives bolted to the hull. This allowed the sprockets to propel the vehicle

M18 Hellcat Tank Destroyer
The rear of the M18 shows its large access door for rolling out the engine when service or replacement was needed. The Continental R975C-4 engine put out 460hp. The ring mount for the .50 caliber machine gun was unique to this vehicle. It was built into the turret itself. Spare track shoes were on the back of the turret bustle. The torsion-bar suspension with its five duel rubber-tired road wheels made its high speed possible. The 76mm gun had the later production muzzle brake on it. In these photos, "Amaz'n Grace" was running; the engine ran so well there was absolutely no exhaust visible. Tom Berndt

M39 Gun Carriage
Sloan and John Upton's M39, serial number 652, sits in the late afternoon sun in northern California. The M39 was an altered M18 Hellcat tank destroyer chassis. After the M18s were built, about 658 were returned to the factory. Turrets were removed, and the superstructure and interior were changed. Its mission *was an armored utility vehicle, but oftentimes it towed an anti-tank gun or performed another role. As can be seen in the photo, the vehicle had tremendous amounts of storage. The unusual ring mount from the M18 turret was used in the front of the crew compartment. A crew of nine served the vehicle. Both the M18 and M39 were built by Buick.* John Upton

over its tracks. The Torqmatic transmission was one of the forerunners of the Allison automatic transmissions in commercial use today.

In World War II, the M18 and M39 used a T69 all-steel, single-pin track with a short pitch sprocket. After World War II, a rubber track and different sprockets were used—the same as those used on the M24 Chaffee light tank track. Five dual rubber-tired road wheels were mounted on torsion bar suspension on each side of the vehicle. Four top return rollers supported the track, with a tensioned steel idler wheel at the rear. The front drive sprocket and road wheel had an extra compensating link to keep the track in place

at high speeds. Sand shields were fitted on some vehicles. On the M18 and M39, each road wheel had a shock absorber. An auxiliary generator was located at the right front of the hull on the floor.

The M39 was actually a modified M18. The turret was removed, and a short superstructure was added around the top of the opening. Storage was changed for the crew of nine. The M39's primary purpose was to tow the 3in M6 anti-tank gun. Two large armored doors were added to the outside sponsons for storage purposes. Seats were added for a crew of eight in the fighting compartment. A ring mount for a .50 caliber machine gun was added at the front of the compartment. Forty-

M39 Gun Carriage
At the rear of the M39 we see additional storage for the 3in M6 gun. Access to the sponson stowage compartments is visible on the center of the hull. The small sheet metal skirts were very effective in keeping dust and dirt down to a minimum. The rear door and ramp for engine service are clearly seen here as well as the special pintle for cross country towing of the gun. Fuel cells were in the engine compartment with the engine's dry sump oiling system. This M39 is fitted with the later rubber chevron tracks also used on the M24 Chaffee light tank. John Upton

two rounds of 3in ammunition, 900 rounds of .50 caliber, 1,620 rounds of .30 caliber carbine ammunition, and grenades were carried. Armor thickness was the same as the M18. An SCR610 radio set was placed in the right sponson. A 24-volt electrical system was provided by a generator driven off the drive-shaft.

The M39 was lighter than the M18 by about 4,000lb. At 35,000lb, it was even faster than the M18. It was 17ft, 4in long, 9ft, 1/2in wide, and 5ft, 11in high to the top of the hull, with a 14in ground clearance. Vertical obstacle ability was 36in and fording depth was 48in.

4

Medium and Heavy Tanks

The M4 series tanks used in World War II were built in greater numbers and more widely used than any other model of their period. The name "Sherman" was, of course, given to it in honor of the famous General Sherman of the US Civil War. It is without a doubt the most recognized name of any tank ever built. This recognition has also made it the most popular tank among collectors in the continental United States. Within the hobby of collecting military vehicles, the Sherman tank is the most sought after piece for one's collection.

M4 Sherman Medium Tank

The M4 had its origins in the 1936 T5 tank. Although the M4 was a completely dif-

M4A1 Sherman Medium Tank
The nice background here shows the tall silhouette of the Sherman hull and turret. This was changed in the later tank designs. Although the applique armor helped protect the ammunition, one can't help wondering if it made a better aiming point for the enemy.
Tom Berndt

ferent vehicle, its basic design and suspension was visible in the T5's appearance. The design was improved as it was tested in the late 1930s and evolved into the M2 series with a different superstructure. More testing was done and more improvements recommended, culminating in the M3 Lee model, a distinctive tank with twin turrets. The larger of the two Lee turrets had a 37mm gun and a coaxial .30 caliber machine gun, as well as a second, smaller commander's turret on top with a .30 caliber machine gun. A 75mm gun was mounted in the right sponson. This mount had limited traverse and eventually proved to be inefficient. This limitation was one of the leading factors in the design of the M4 with its larger single turret, which revolved a full 360deg and had either power or manual control.

The first M3s had riveted hulls and were built in August 1941; by August 1942, 4,924 had been manufactured. Some had redesigned turrets and were sent to England under Lend-Lease programs.

The M3's successor was the M3A1, which was the same for the most part, but had a cast hull rather than a riveted hull. An M3A2 followed with an all-welded hull. The M3A3 was also a welded-hull tank and had twin 6-71 GMC diesel engines. The M3A5 was the same as an M3A3 but had a riveted hull. The M3A4 had an experimental 30-cylinder Chrysler multibank engine installed in November 1941, with a longer hull to accept this larger engine. The engine was basically a group of five car engines designed to run as one. Not many M3A4s were built, but the engine proved successful and was put into the M4A4 in the M4 series.

The M3 series was used extensively in North Africa before being replaced by the new M4s. A few were used in the Pacific as well. M3s were given to England, France, Russia, and Canada. Even Canada built M3s modified for British use, called the Ram series. These models had a completely different turret and superstructure.

The M4 series began in December 1941 with a welded hull. In February 1942, a cast-hull model was put into production. Three

M4A1E8 Sherman Medium Tank
The bright sunlight shows the smooth castings of the hull, differential, and turret of Henry Vendetta's restored M4A1E8 Sherman, built by Baldwin Locomotive, serial number 3360. This vehicle is an exquisite example of a restored tank. The interior is as beautiful as the exterior, complete with all stowage, munitions, spare parts, crew equipment, and
accessories; and it runs as good as it looks. The length of the more powerful 76mm gun can be seen here. This tank has the wet stowage ammunition bins that carried 71 rounds of high explosive, armor-piercing, and smoke for the M1A1 or M1A2 main gun. With a muzzle velocity of 2,600ft per second, penetration was 4in of armor at 1,000ft. Tom Berndt

companies built the M4A1: Pacific Car and Foundry, Lima Locomotive Works, and Pressed Steel Car Company. Production ceased in September, November, and December 1943 for the three companies, respectively. The M4A1s with the 75mm gun were numerous, with total production at 6,281 units.

Five companies eventually built the M4 welded-hull models: American Locomotive, Detroit Tank Arsenal, Pullman Standard Car Company, Baldwin Locomotive Works, and Pressed Steel Car Company. With a total of 6,748 vehicles manufactured, the total M4

and M4A1 production figures came to 13,029. Production ceased at Pressed Steel Car in January 1944.

The next model was the M4A2. This unit had twin 6-71 Detroit Diesel engines. The exterior was made up of an all-welded hull, cast turret 75mm gun, and a one-piece cast differential housing. Production began in September 1942 and ended in May 1944. A total of 8,053 units were built by five manufacturers: Fisher Tank Arsenal, Pullman Standard Car Company, American Locomotive, Baldwin Locomotive Works, and Federal Machine and

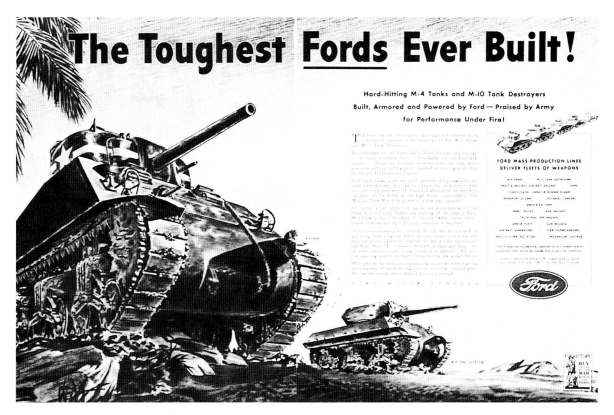

M4 and M10 Tank Ad
"The Toughest Fords Ever Built!"

M4A1E8 Sherman Medium Tank
Detail of the sharp-nosed differential and accessories of this tank. The gun-traveling lock, headlights, bow mount, and other items can be seen clearly here. On
the mantlet, snaps can clearly be seen for the canvas dust cover. A completely new turret was used on the E8 series of Shermans with all-new wider tracks and better suspension. Tom Berndt

Welder Company. The M4A2 was given to England and Russia under Lend-Lease. The US forces used them mostly in training in the United States; a few were used in Okinawa and Tunisia.

The M4A3 was the most favored of the models because of its powerplant, the Ford GAA liquid-cooled V-8. The design was begun in the late 1930s as an aircraft engine in V-12 configuration and the GAA V-8 had the

appearance of the V-12 except that it had four of all components on each side.

May 1942 was the introduction date of the M4A3 built by Ford. In Ford's first production run from June 1942 to September 1943, 1,690 M4A3s were built. The basic tank was the same as the M4 with a welded hull, narrow tracks, and cast differential housing. The engine compartment had some rearrangements for the engine change, but the majority of the components were the same as the other models. This model used the 75mm gun with dry ammunition storage. Several thousand more were built with wet stowage for the 75mm gun and the higher-velocity 76mm gun during the period from February 1944 to April 1945.

M4A4s were a most fascinating tank. The hull was lengthened and the Chrysler A57 multibank engine was installed. All the M4s and M4A1s had radials, as did most of the M2 and M3 series vehicles, but during World War II, radial engine production facilities were needed for aircraft engines so alternative powerplants were designed and tested.

The A57 multibank was a combination of five Chrysler industrial L-head six-cylinder gasoline engines built to run as one. The engine blocks were bolted to a common crankcase with a dry-sump oiling system. Each engine crankshaft had a small gear on it, rather than a flywheel, that ran a large sun gear, which in turn had a clutch and flywheel assembly behind it. Five carburetors and dis-

M4A1E8 Sherman Medium Tank
The horizontal volute spring suspension is visible here. The wider track still used the double sprockets, engaging the outside of the end connectors. But a box-type center guide was now used with the dual-tired *road wheels. This track was 23in wide. Spare track blocks sit on top of the side fenders. The massive rear turret bustle shows the anti-aircraft gun mount.*
Tom Berndt

tributors were used and many of the engine accessories and housings were altered for this installation. It really was a 30-cylinder engine.

Chrysler built 7,499 M4A4s from July 1942 to September 1943. US forces never used M4A4s in combat, but some were kept as trainers in the United States. Thousands were sent overseas to England and China.

M4A4s were built with the three-piece differential housing, welded hull, and 75mm dry storage gun. Narrow tracks and vertical volute suspension carried the vehicle. Only one running M4A4 is known to remain in existence, in St. Paul, Minnesota; another M4A4 is at the Aberdeen Proving Grounds in Maryland; and an A57 engine is on display at the Ellingson Car Museum in Rogers, Minnesota.

The M4A6 was the last model to be built and standardized. Some seventy-five units were assembled, but the program was dropped due to the end of the war. It was an M4A4 design, but had a Wright G200 air-cooled radial that was converted to diesel configuration by Caterpillar Tractor Company. It put out 450hp at 2000 rpm, but had an astounding 1470lb-ft of torque at 1200rpm. The ordnance model number for the engine was the RD1820.

M4A1E8 Sherman Medium Tank
Ready to shoot, the M4A1E8 comes out of the woods looking for action. It was 104 degrees on the day this tank was photographed—can you imagine how hot it was inside the hull with all the hatches closed? Luckily, the air-cooled radial engine draws a tremendous amount of air through the fighting compartment. Unfortunately, in a restored vehicle such as this, it also draws in dust, dirt, and everything else airborne. Keeping the interior clean is a real effort.
Tom Berndt

The standard powerplants in the M4 series Shermans were as follows:

M4 and M4A1: Continental R975-C-1 of 973ci, 400hp at 2400 rpm, 890lb-ft of torque at 1800rpm. Air-cooled, radial design. 1,137lb dry weight. Later models used the R975-C-4 with 460hp.

M4A2: General Motors two-cycle diesel 6046 had two 6-71 inline engines tied together with a transfer case: 850ci, liquid cooled, 410hp at 2900rpm, 885lb-ft of torque at 1900rpm. 5,110lb dry weight.

M4A3: Ford GAA V-8 gasoline: 1100ci, 500hp at 2600rpm, 1,040lb-ft of torque at 2200rpm. Aluminum block, overhead camshafts. Magneto ignition. 1,560lb dry weight.

M4A4: Chrysler A57 multibank: liquid-cooled, gasoline-fired, 1253ci, 425hp at 2850rpm, 1,060lb-ft of torque at 1400rpm. 30 cylinders. 5,400lb dry weight.

M4A6: Ordnance RD1820 radial, air-cooled diesel. Nine-cylinder, 1823ci, 450hp at 2000rpm, 1,470lb-ft of torque at 1200rpm. 3,536lb dry weight.

Other experimental engines were tried. Guiberson tried a radial diesel. Chrysler tried a V-12 liquid-cooled model called the A65, which had 650hp from 1568ci. General Motors tried a liquid-cooled V-8-184 diesel, which was half of a V-16 used in a ship. Lycoming tied three flat-opposed, air-cooled gasoline aircraft engines together and called it the T1300, with 560hp from 1,300ci.

M4A1 Sherman Medium Tank
Jacques Littlefield's early M4A1 sits in a meadow reminiscent of northern Italy in the summer. The standard 75mm gun is seen here with the later *mantlet. The applique armor on the side of the hull was added protection for the ammunition racks inside.* Tom Berndt

M4 Sherman Ad
"Oldsmobile's on the offensive!"

The M4 series transmission and differential were all pretty much the same. A five-speed manual transmission was bolted directly to the differential at the front of the vehicle. Fifth gear was overdrive. Two levers were used to steer the tank. These activated brakes on bands, oil bathed in the controlled differential. Three differential housings were used: a three-piece bolt-together, a cast-nose one-piece, and a later one called a "sharp nose" cast housing, which eventually replaced all the others.

Drive sprockets at the front, mounted on the final drives, propelled the Shermans over two basic types of tracks and suspension. The first type was a vertical volute spring design with three bogie clusters on each side. Each cluster had two rubber-tired bogie wheels. Five different types of bogie wheels were used throughout the production. Top return rollers and an adjustable rear idler wheel complemented the track design. The second design was called the horizontal volute spring suspension. These were larger bogie clusters, but still had three on each side of the tank. Shock absorbers were used with four wheels per cluster.

The 23in-wide track used a center guide rather than the outside end connector guides used on the narrower 16 1/2in track. Both narrow and wide track came in a variety of types: steel or rubber chevron, smooth rubber block, or intermittent bar cleat in the narrow design. The steel or rubber chevron came in the wider 23in type. The wide-track vehicles were called the "easy eights." An E8 designation was added to each model number that had the new, wider tracks and suspension.

Many weapons systems were employed, but the basic systems were two similar guns. Early vehicles used the 75mm gun with wet or dry storage. Later vehicles used a high-velocity 76mm with a longer barrel in a new larger turret. All 76mm guns used wet-type storage. All models had a .30 caliber bow-mounted machine gun operated by the assistant driver. A .30 caliber machine gun was coaxially mounted with the main gun, and a .50 caliber machine gun was placed on the outside of the turret for anti-aircraft use.

The M4 series tanks weighed nearly twice as much as the light tanks. Gross weight or combat fighting weight was 66,500lb on the M4 and M4A1, 69,000lb on the M4A2, 68,500lb on the M4A3, and 71,000lb on the M4A4 and M4A6.

The M4's armor thicknesses were as follows: 2in hull upper front; 1 1/2in to 2in lower front; 1 1/2in to 2in sides; 1 1/2in rear; 1in top; 1/2in to 1in bottom, depending upon the area; 3in front turret armor; 2in side turret armor; and 1in top turret armor. The "jumbo" or M4A3E2 was considerably heavier. The jumbo's armor was thicker, with 6in turret front, sides and rear, and 1in turret top. The gun shield was 7in thick. Hull upper front was 4in; lower was 4 1/2in to 5 1/2in. Hull sides were 3in. Other areas remained the same. The weight went up to 84,000lb gross, and this extra weight required lower gearing in the final drives. Speed was reduced to 22mph, where other models were 24–29mph on level roads.

All the Sherman hulls were between 19ft and 20ft long; width on the narrow-tracked vehicles was 8ft, 7in wide.

M4A1 Sherman Medium Tank
The American armored hero of World War II, the M4 Sherman tank. This early M4A1 was fitted with the standard 75mm gunm seen here with the later mantlet. This M4A1 is owned by Jacques Littlefield. Tom Berndt

M4A4 Sherman Medium Tank
M4A4 Shermans are incredibly rare. Here is a stunning example of serial number 5598, belonging to George Rabuse and his son, Grant. One other is known of at Aberdeen Proving Grounds in Maryland. This unit is in running condition with all of its original equipment. When found, it had been kept indoors for nearly forty years and was in excellent condition. It is particularly interesting that this vehicle is almost as it left the factory, with few British modifications. The A57 multibank is a most fascinating engine to hear run. Grant Rabuse

Gradeability was 60 percent on all models; they could climb a 24in vertical obstacle. Trench crossing ability was 8ft, 5in. Fording depths were 36in to 42in, depending on the model. Fuel capacities were 148gal to 175gal, which gave various models a 100–150-mile cruising range.

Radio communications were in the rear of the turrets with interphone stations for all crew members. A variety of radios were carried: SCR506, 508, 528, and 538. A hand signal flag set was standard in all tanks. All M4 Sherman vehicles used a 24-volt electrical system.

The M4 series tank and chassis were used for numerous other types of vehicles. Prime movers were used to tow heavy artillery components. These were essentially tanks without turrets. Self-propelled artillery were built on modified chassis with different superstructures; 105mm, 155mm, and 8in guns were used. A large number of gun motor carriages were built for antitank use. These had open top turrets and extensive hull modifications for better ballistics. Three-inch and 90mm guns made these units effective weapons. The M4A3E2 assault tank, called the "jumbo," was built with much thicker armor for the engagement of the Siegfried Line. A larger series of recovery vehicles were built with a huge winch on the center floor of the tank and a dummy turret above it. These winches usually had a 60,000–90,000lb capacity. A huge A-frame-type boom was used for lifting. Flame-thrower tanks were built with the components inside the vehicle.

Countless other experiments and devices were conducted with these chassis. Flotation and fording equipment was designed to make the vehicle amphibious. Mine-clearing tanks, as well as self-propelled anti-aircraft guns, were tried. Engineer vehicles with dozer blades, rocket launchers on top of turrets, bridging equipment for large ditches or small streams, and mortar carriers with large-displacement mortars fired from the vehicle were just a few of the modications tested.

M4A4 Sherman Medium Tank
George and Grant Rabuse have nearly completed a beautiful restoration of their A57 multibank engine. This unit is a later model with the large single water pump and five carburetors on top for ease of

maintenance. The red ignition coils set off the colors nicely, with the huge radiator behind the engine. The powerplant, radiator, and clutch housing all come out in one unit. It practically runs and services itself. It is an intriguing feat of engineering. Tom Berndt

Countless engine, transmission, suspension, armor, armament, and weapons systems were experimented with. Tanks given to the British often had further weapons and communications modifications done to them. In all, over 72,400 tanks and chassis were built during World War II using the M4 series for various purposes. By the time production ended in 1945, the last tanks were almost completely different than the first because so many changes were made.

M26 Pershing Medium-Heavy Tank

The M26 Pershing was the most modern tank design the United States developed in World War II. Designs began in December 1942 with the idea of using all the most modern innovations in powertrain, suspension, armor, and weaponry.

The M26 was originally designated a medium tank, then a heavy tank, and back to a medium tank just after the war. Production took place at Detroit Tank Arsenal, operated by Chrysler, and Grand Blanc Tank Arsenal, operated by Fisher Body Division of General Motors. General Motors built 1,190 Pershings between November 1944 and June 1945. An additional 992 were produced by Detroit Arsenal in late 1945.

The M26 Pershing design was all new for a US tank. Many of the lessons learned early in World War II combat were considered and applied to the production of this vehicle.

As with the medium tanks of the time, the Pershing's combat interior design was quite similar. The hull of the vehicle was a combination of welded armor plate and castings. Commander and gunner sat on the right side of the turret with one in front of the other. The commander's cupola was similar to the late Sherman tanks, with a periscope in the hatch and a series of vision blocks around the base of the hatch.

M4A1E8 Sherman Medium Tank
The Wright Military Museum's M4A1E8 Sherman, built by Fisher Body Division of General Motors. This front view shows its massive size from a close

"foxhole" perspective. Note the early gun tube without a muzzle brake. The wider tracks of the E8 tanks really helped their flotation on soft ground. Tom Berndt

The loader was on the right side of the turret with a top hatch for entrance and a small side hatch on the right side of the turret for ejection of empty shell casings.

Main armament was a high-velocity Model M3 90mm gun with a coaxially mounted .30 caliber machine gun on the left side. A .50 caliber M2 mounted on the roof for anti-aircraft use. The rear of the turret was the traditional mount for the radio sets. Sev-

eral models were used: SCR508, 528, or 608B, British #19 set, or AN/VRC3 were used in different vehicles. Five interphone stations were provided for crew members.

The gun mount was an M67 combination unit and used a telescopic-sight M71C and a M10F periscope. Ammunition was carried in the floor in four bins surrounded by thin water tanks, which would supposedly extinguish a fire if the bins were penetrated. Sever-

M4A3E8 Sherman Medium Tank
This old M4A3E8 hull sat upside down on its turret top for twenty-five years. Although tough in appearance, the interior was clean and easily restored.

It is interesting to see a vehicle with the front differential housing off. Sherman parts are not that uncommon. Tom Berndt

al rounds were carried in the ready rack on the left side of the turret. The turret didn't have a basket as older tanks did; instead, it had three crew members in their seats, ready rack ammunition, and hydraulic systems that traversed with the turret itself. Turret movement was by power hydraulic or manual control.

Below and in front of the turret were the driver's position on the left and assistant driver's position on the right. Both the driver and assistant had a set of controls. Each side had steering brake levers for the mechanically controlled differential, an accelerator pedal for engine speed, a manual throttle control, and a speed range selector with safety lock for the Torqmatic transmission. Accelerator and speed range controls used cables, and the steering linkages were all mechanical on the bottom of the tank hull.

The assistant driver had a bow-mounted .30 caliber machine gun, with 5,000 rounds of .30 caliber ammunition on board. Additional ammunition included 550 rounds of .50 cal-

M4A3E8 Sherman Medium Tank
The M4A3E8 had the all-welded hull made of flat armor plate. With some of the items missing on the front of this vehicle, you can see the good slope of the glacia plate. This unit awaits restoration. Tom Berndt

iber for the outside anti-aircraft gun, along with 900 rounds of .45 caliber for the five M3 submachine guns of the crew.

The hull of the vehicle was a welded assembly, made up of rolled plates and castings. The turret was a single casting. All the steel used was homogeneous. The hull front armor had 4in upper and 3in lower thicknesses. Side thicknesses were 3in in front and 2in in rear. Rear thickness varied from 3/4in to 2in. Bottom front of the vehicle had a 1in thickness; bottom rear had a 1/2in thickness.

M32B3 Tank Retriever
This M32B3 tank retriever is truly a rare vehicle. Found in the midwest some years ago, it is the Wright Military Museum's main workhorse. It was built out of an early M4A3 hull and cast differential. Late solid bogie wheels are used with the late production heavy bogie clusters. The main winch had a 60,000lb capacity and was mounted on the floor directly under the turret. The cable came through the fair lead in the front of the hull for straight line pulling. The cable could be restrung through the top of the dummy turret for use with the boom. An 81mm mortar was mounted on the outside of the hull in the front center. Hull and chassis specifications and components were the same as the tanks themselves. Tom Berndt

M7B1 Priest

This beautiful example of an M7B1 Priest, owned by Jacque Littlefield and done in rich darker olive drab, is a rare vehicle. The production quantities of self-propelled artillery on Sherman chassis was low in comparison to the tanks themselves. Only 826 M7B1s were built from March 1944 to February 1945. This vehicle has a Ford GAA V-8 powertrain and mounts a 105mm Howitzer. M7s had the M4A1 chassis with the radial engine. The M7's superstructure and "pulpit" were shorter in height than the M7B1. Tom Berndt

M7B1 Priest
Here the Priest is moving to the meadow. The driver
sits behind the open hatch in the left front. As can be
seen in this photo, the superstructure above the tracks
is completely different than the tanks themselves. Even
on dry ground the dust churned up by the tracks is
incredible and gets the dark paint dirty instantly.
Tom Berndt

The turret armor thickness included a 4in front, 3in sides, a 3in rear, a 1in top, and a 4 1/2in gun shield.

The suspension of the M26 was a dramatic improvement over the horizontal volute spring suspension or vertical volute spring suspension of the M4 Sherman series. Each set of six road wheels was attached to a tor-sion bar mounted in the bottom of the hull. This provided a smooth ride and exceptional cross-country performance. Top return rollers supported the track with the adjustable idler at the front of the vehicle. The drive sprockets were at the rear. The two front and two rear road wheels on each side had double-acting shock absorbers. A 24in single-pin steel or

M7B1 Priest

A good side view of the Priest shows the reason for its nickname—the pulpit-like armored shield of the anti-aircraft mount for the .50 caliber machine gun. The howitzer can be seen overhanging the front armor.

This gun was the standard M2A1 with its carriage modified and welded right inside the chassis. A high-explosive shell has a muzzle velocity of 1,550ft per second and a maximum range of 12,200yds.
Tom Berndt

M7B1 Priest

This tube on the 105mm gun is an early model. Although it is countersunk to prevent the muzzle from splitting, it does not have the heavier muzzle collar of the later tubes. The recoil cylinder is on top with the fitting in the end for replenishing the hydraulic oil when needed. The recoil tube was made of seamless tubing. Tom Berndt

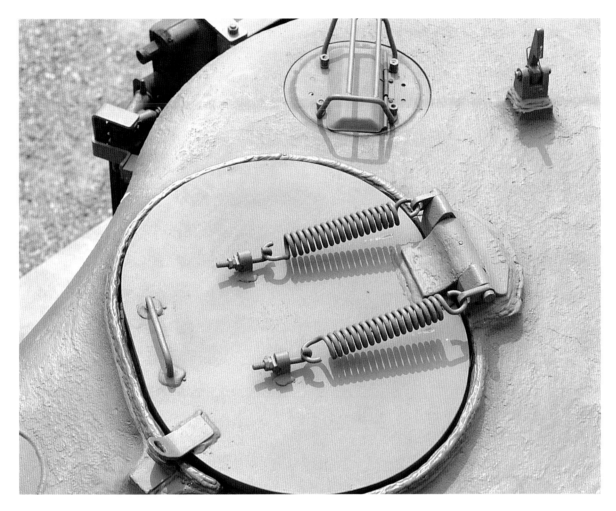

M4A1E8 Sherman Medium Tank
The loader's hatch, which was standard on all the 76mm turrets, was a welcome safety feature for the loader. He now had his own escape route, whereas before, he had to go over or under the gun, following the commander and gunner out the commander's hatch. This time lapse in escape in earlier turrets proved to be fatal to many loaders. Tom Berndt

23in double-pin rubber track were used, with a center guide in each shoe. The tracks were covered with full fenders front to rear; three large storage boxes sat on the top of each fender.

The engine used in the M26 was a GAF 500hp Ford V-8—a slightly modified GAA design, adapted to the torqmatic transmission and controlled differential assembly. The engine sat just behind the fighting compartment bulkhead beneath the rear of the turret. On each side was a 92gal fuel tank. To the rear of the right fuel tank was the water-cooled auxiliary engine and 24-volt generator. The gen-

M4A1E8 Sherman Medium Tank
Pistol ports, as they were called, were used for ejecting empty shell casings. This one on the side of David

Wright's M4A1E8 shows good detail of the casting.
Tom Berndt

M4A3 Sherman Medium Tank
Stainless-steel rod was used to weld the tank hulls. This applique shield added to Frank Buck's M4A3 is attached with numerous beads of weld. Note the weld

of the front glacia plate to the side armor in the left corner of the photo below the track guides and lip for the sand shields. Tom Berndt

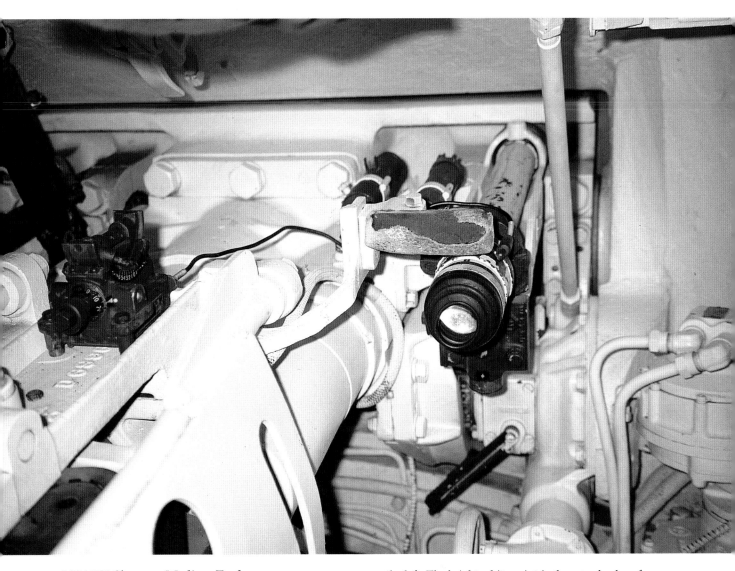

M4A1E8 Sherman Medium Tank
The gunner's position in Henry Venetta's M4A1E8 shows the M71D telescopic sight. At the right is the top of the turret hydraulic motor. The breech shield is on the left. The bright white paint is the actual color of a new Sherman interior. The entire gun assembly is held in place in the M67 mount. Henry Venetta

erator could be run by the main engine or the auxiliary. Air cleaners and oil filters were at the front of the engine. The engine's magnetos were at its front, and the carburetors were at the front and rear of the intake manifold. At the rear corners of the engine were the radiators, one on each side, with propeller shaft-driven fans. A planetary reduction gear

M4A1E8 Sherman Medium Tank
Looking down the commander's hatch opening, we see the folded commander's seat and the gunner's seat below it. A binocular case and interior light sit on the *edge of the turret base ring. Below are water cans and a fire extinguisher pull handle. Part of the interphone system and turret electrical system are in the box next to the binoculars.* Henry Venetta

case, then the torque converter, and then the planetary transmission gear case were attached to the rear of the engine. These were all bolted together and attached to the me-

chanically controlled differential. Small driveshafts sent the power out to the side-mounted planetary final drives at the rear corners of the tank's hull. Although it seems like a long combination, the engine, transmission, and differential were quite compact and could be removed as one unit.

The engine compartment had a fixed fire extinguisher system to suppress fuel, oil, or explosive fires. The exhaust system ran straight out the back in the center of the rear plate, with the gun traveling track just above it. The engine compartment was covered with armored louvered intake and exhaust grates, which served as engine covers as well.

The tank's exterior had standard military items: front and rear tow shackles and cable, 24-volt headlights, siren, and armored tail-

M4A1 Sherman Medium Tank
The sun lights up the front of Jacques Littlefield's M4A1 hull. The armored ventilator is at the upper left. The pedestal-type headlights are removed, and a replica .30 caliber gun looks good. The travel-lock brackets and snap heads for the canvas bow-mount cover are clearly seen. At the bottom, the assembly of the three-piece differential housing is evident. The casting of the hull was very smooth on US tanks. World War II Russian vehicles were unbelievably crude. Extensive grinding was often done on US hulls, and Russian ones were sometimes flame-trimmed with a torch. German tanks were built almost entirely of flat plate. Tom Berndt

M4A3 Sherman Medium Tank

This close-up shows Frank Buck's M4A3 early mantlet and M34 gun mount from an extremely early tank in the series. It is hard to believe it was not replaced with the wider M34A1 shield of later vehicles. At the bottom of the photo, we see additional plate welded in front of the hatch openings and a periscope shield. The gun in this tank is the 75mm M3 gun, which was used in most early Shermans. Tom Berndt

lights. Spare track sections were carried on the turret with storage for miscellaneous items.

The M26's power plant and gear train gave its 92,000lb weight a top sustained

T26E3/M26 Pershing Medium-Heavy Tank

This side view of Wright Museum's M26 tank shows the total redesign of the US tank after the Sherman. Everything was new, improved, and more efficient: 90mm gun, rear engine with rear transmission and differential, and all new torsion bar suspension. The M26 Pershing was a real match for the German tanks. Note the rear travel lock for the gun just above the exhaust outlets. Tom Berndt

T26E3/M26 Pershing Medium-Heavy Tank
The rear turret bustle on the M26 Pershing was even larger than the late Sherman turret. The hull of this tank is made up of a combination of flat plate and castings. The turret is a one-piece casting.
Tom Berndt

speed of 25mph on level road. The long length of track on the ground provided a low 12.7psi ground pressure, and it was capable of crossing an 8ft trench. Vertical obstacle ability was 46in, and a 4ft fording depth could be attained without preparation.

T26E3/M26 Pershing Medium-Heavy Tank

David Wright's magnificent T26E3 Pershing, serial number 35, rests in a more peaceful yard than it did in World War II. This is an early Pershing that actually fought at the Bridge of Remagen. It is probably one of the most unique tanks in private hands in the United States. It is rare that a combat-used vehicle ever comes back from overseas. There are a few others like this in the United States: Fred Ropkey has a M24 Chaffee that was a Japanese Self-Defense Force vehicle. It was shipped to Korea for the conflict, captured by the North Koreans, and used against US forces. Then it was recaptured by US forces, reused against the North Koreans, and somehow found its way back to the United States. Its history was discovered when the tank was repainted. A new coat of paint was applied over the North Korean markings to preserve it. Some of the stories are astounding to say the least.

Tom Berndt

M26 Pershing Medium-Heavy Tank
Fred Ropkey's M26 Pershing is done in Korean War dark olive drab. This vehicle got a complete restoration.

Note the German Sturmgeschütz in the background.
Tom Berndt

The body length of the hull overall was 249in, width was 138in, and height to the top of the turret was 109in.

A total of 310 units were shipped to Europe in early to mid-1945. Only twenty actu-ally saw combat. None ever faced a King Tiger, although some saw action with Tiger Mk Is, Panthers, and Panzer Mk IVs. Two pla-toons fought at the Bridge of Remagen. A few went to Okinawa but never saw action.

T26E3/M26 Pershing Medium-Heavy Tank
The Pershing's silhouette was very different than the

Sherman's—much lower and sleeker. We see here there is almost no hull visible above the tracks. Tom Berndt

Index